Cool Hotels
Australia/Pacific

edited by
Martin Nicholas Kunz

teNeues

Imprint

Produced by fusion publishing GmbH, Berlin, www.fusion-publishing.com

Editorial team: Martin Nicholas Kunz (Editor + Layout)
Lea Bauer (Editorial coordination)
Constanze Junker (Introduction, "What's special" texts)
Sabine Scholz (Text coordination), ASCO International Translations (Translation)
Janine Minkner, Jan Hausberg, Peter Fritzsche (Prepress + Imaging)
Cover photo (location): Barbara Kraft (Four Seasons Resort Bora Bora)
Back cover photos from top to bottom (location): Courtesy The Farm at Cape Kidnappers (The Farm at Cape Kidnappers);
courtesy The Byron at Byron Bay Resort and Spa (The Byron at Byron Resort and Spa); courtesy Cradle Mountain Lodge (Cradle
Mountain Lodge); courtesy Royal Davui Island Resort (Royal Davui Island Resort); courtesy Vatulele Island Resort (Vatulele
Island Resort)

Photos (location): Bill Bachman (Whare Kea Lodge); Markus Bachmann (Crown Promenade Hotel, Hotel Lindrum, The
Prince, The Hatton); courtesy Blanket Bay (Blanket Bay); courtesy BLUE Sydney, A Taj Hotel (BLUE Sydney, A Taj Hotel);
courtesy Jointly The Buckland - Studio Retreat and Jamie Durant (The Buckland - Studio Retreat); courtesy The Byron
at Byron Bay Resort and Spa (The Byron at Byron Resort and Spa); courtesy Cradle Mountain Lodge (Cradle Mountain
Lodge); courtesy Delamore Lodge (Delamore Lodge); courtesy Design Hotels™ (Limes Hotel); courtesy Diamant
Boutique Hotel Canberra (Diamant Boutique Hotel Canberra); courtesy Eagles Nest (Eagles Nest); Photographer: Earl
Carter, Copyright: Wesley Douvos (Olive Grove Retreat); courtesy Eichardt's Private Hotel (Eichardt's Private Hotel);
courtesy The Farm at Cape Kidnappers (The Farm at Cape Kidnappers); Murray Fredericks (Establishment); Ethan
Gordon (The Wakaya Club & Spa; Four Seasons Resort Bora Bora); Loic Le Guilly (The Islington Hotel); courtesy The
Henry Jones Art Hotel (The Henry Jones Art Hotel); courtesy Jean-Michel Cousteau Fiji Islands Resort (Jean-Michel Cousteau
Fiji Islands Resort); Barbara Kraft (The Wakaya Club & Spa); Martin Nicholas Kunz (Hilton Moorea Lagoon Resort & Spa,
Intercontinental Resort Tahiti); courtesy The Lodge at Kauri Cliffs (The Lodge at Kauri Cliffs); courtesy The Lodge at Tarraleah
(The Lodge at Tarraleah); courtesy Longitude 131 (Longitude 131); Chris McClennan (Jean-Michel Cousteau Fiji Islands Resort);
courtesy Mollies on Tweed (Mollies on Tweed); courtesy Moonlight Head Private Lodge (Moonlight Head Private Lodge); Jona-
than Phillips (Le Méridien Bora Bora); courtesy The Quadrant (THE QUADRANT HOTEL AUCKLAND); Gilbert van Reenen (Whare
Kea Lodge); courtesy River Birches Lodge (River Birches Lodge); Moeava de Rosemont (Four Seasons Resort Bora Bora); Barbara
Rowell (Jean-Michel Cousteau Fiji Islands Resort); courtesy Royal Davui Island Resort (Royal Davui Island Resort); Three Loose
Coconuts (The Wakaya Club & Spa); courtesy Treetops Lodge (Treetops Lodge); courtesy Vatulele Island Resort (Vatulele Island
Resort); courtesy Wakaya Club (The Wakaya Club & Spa); James Walshe (Jean-Michel Cousteau Fiji Islands Resort); Courtesy
Wilson Island (Wilson Island)

Price orientation: $ = < 200 $, $$ = 201 $ − 350 $, $$$ = 351 $ − 550 $, $$$$ = > 551 $

Published by teNeues Publishing Group

teNeues Verlag GmbH + Co. KG	teNeues Publishing Company	teNeues Publishing UK Ltd.
Am Selder 37	16 West 22nd Street	York Villa, York Road
47906 Kempen, Germany	New York, NY 10010, USA	Byfleet, KT14 7HX,
Tel.: 0049-(0)2152-916-0	Tel.: 001-212-627-9090	Great Britain
Fax: 0049-(0)2152-916-111	Fax: 001-212-627-9511	Tel.: 0044-1932-403509
E-mail: books@teneues.de		Fax: 0044-1932-403514

teNeues France S.A.R.L.
93, rue Bannier
45000 Orléans, France
Tel.: 0033-2-38541071
Fax: 0033-2-38625340

Press department: arehn@teneues.de
Tel.: 0049-(0)2152-916-202

www.teneues.com

ISBN: 978-3-8327-9309-8

Bibliographic information published by the Deutsche Nationalbibliothek.
The Deutsche Nationalbibliothek lists this publication in the Deutsche Nationalbibliografie;
detailed bibliographic data are available in the Internet at http://dnb.d-nb.de

Contents
Page

Introduction

Australia, New Zealand, the South Seas – breathtaking climes in the southern hemisphere. Each itself a place of dreams and longing and for many people, paradise at the other end of the world.

But the long trip there is worth it. Tropical rainforests and uninhabited deserts, endless beaches and the world's largest coral reef, remote cattle ranches, deserted gold mining towns and bustling metropolises – at the latest, sometime between four and five PM when at Magic Hour the sun bathes the countryside in a mystical, surreal light, one succumbs to Australia's fascination, this unbelievable land of contrasts and superlatives.

With its unique flora and fauna the fabulous wilderness of New Zealand lures as well. A third of the country is under environmental protection and is like a wonderland in which time has stood still.

The exoticism of picturesque lagoons and the luxuriant flowers of Polynesia transport every-one into a seemingly perpetual and cheerful serenity, the ease of simply being.

The selection of exclusive hotels, lodges und resorts here are sublime complements to these extraordinary destinations. Style, comfort and technique combine historical cities, ar-chaic wilderness or remote dreams of nature with the modernity of our times, create breath-taking vistas and at the same time maintain the singular romanticism of these refuges.

Between the poles of exceptional, modern architecture or historical hulls of buildings and sportive interiors or straightforward elegance behind the façade, these hospitable establish-ments fulfill the expectations of their exacting guests. This book will help you make your dreams come true by introducing you to the most beautiful hotels of this charming region.

Constanze Junker

Einleitung

Australien, Neuseeland, die Südsee – atemberaubende Gefilde auf der südlichen Hemisphäre. Jeder für sich ein Ort der Träume und Sehnsüchte und für viele Menschen das Paradies am anderen Ende der Welt.

Doch die weite Reise dorthin lohnt sich. Tropische Regenwälder und menschenleere Wüsten, endlose Strände und das größte Korallenriff der Welt, entlegene Viehfarmen, verlassene Goldgräberstädte und geschäftige Metropolen – spätestens, wenn irgendwann zwischen vier und fünf Uhr die Sonne zur *Magic Hour* die Landschaft in ein mystisches, unwirkliches Licht taucht, erliegt man der Faszination Australiens, dieses unglaublichen Landes der Kontraste und Superlative.

Mit seiner einzigartigen Flora und Fauna lockt aber auch die märchenhafte Wildnis Neuseelands, das zu einem Drittel unter Naturschutz steht und wie ein aus der Zeit gefallenes Zauberland wirkt.

Die Exotik der malerischen Lagunen und üppigen tropischen Blumen Polynesiens entrückt hingegen in scheinbar immerwährende heitere Gelassenheit, die Leichtigkeit des Seins.

Die hier ausgewählten exklusiven Hotels, Lodges und Resorts sind sublime Komplemente dieser außergewöhnlichen Reiseziele. Stil, Komfort und Technik verbinden historische Städte, archaische Wildnis oder entlegene Naturträume mit der Modernität unserer Zeit, schaffen atemberaubende Ausblicke und bewahren gleichzeitig die einzigartige Romantik dieser Refugien. In dem Spannungsfeld zwischen außergewöhnlicher, moderner Architektur oder historischer Bauhülle und verspieltem Interieur oder geradliniger Eleganz hinter der Fassade erfüllen diese gastlichen Häuser die Erwartungen ihrer anspruchsvollen Gäste.

Dieses Buch hilft Ihnen, Ihre Träume zu verwirklichen, indem es Ihnen die schönsten Hotels dieser reizvollen Region vorstellt.

Constanze Junker

Introduction

L'Australie, la Nouvelle-Zélande, les Mers du Sud – des paysages de l'hémisphère sud à vous couper le souffle, chacun d'eux un lieu de rêves et de nostalgies. Et pour beaucoup le paradis du bout du monde.

Mais le voyage large en vaut la peine. Forêts équatoriale tropicales et déserts, plages sans fin et la plus grande barrière de corail du monde, des exploitations d'élevage de bétail éparses, des villes de chercheurs d'or abandonnées et des métropoles palpitantes. Au plus tard entre quatre et cinq heures, lorsque le soleil plonge pendant la *Magic Hour* le paysage dans une lumière mystique et irréelle, on succombe à la fascination de l'Australie, ce pays des incroyables contrastes et superlatifs.

Avec ses régions sauvages féeriques, la Nouvelle-Zélande également séduit par sa flore et sa faune uniques, dont un tiers est placé sous protection, et semble un pays magique sorti du temps.

Les lagunes exotiques pittoresques, les exubérantes fleurs tropicales de Polynésie exhalent par contre la légèreté de l'existence par leur sempiternelle impassibilité enjouée. Les hôtels, bungalows et villages touristiques exclusifs sélectionnés ici sont les sublimes complé- ments de ces destinations inhabituelles. Le style, le confort et la technique réunissent villes historiques, lieux sauvages archaïques ou rêves de nature perdue avec la modernité de notre époque, et créent ainsi des paysages à couper le souffle qui gardent en même temps l'ambiance romantique unique de ces refuges. Ces maisons accueillantes situées à la croisée des chemins entre l'architecture inhabituelle, moderne et les intérieurs badins ou l'élégance rectiligne derrière des façades historique, comblent les souhaits des hôtes les plus exigeants. Ce livre vous aidera à réaliser vos rêves, en vous présentant les plus beaux hôtels de cette charmante région.

Constanze Junker

Introducción

Australia, Nueva Zelanda, Oceanía –impresionantes campiñas en el hemisferio sur, cada uno por sí mismo un lugar de sueños y añoranzas. Y para mucha gente el paraíso en el otro extremo del mundo.

Aún el largo viaje hacia allí vale la pena. Selvas tropicales y desiertos despoblados, playas infinitas y el arrecife de corales más grande del mundo, apartadas haciendas de ganado, abandonadas ciudades de buscadores de oro y metrópolis comerciales –a más tardar cuando en algún momento entre las cuatro y las cinco el sol a la *Magic Hour* sumerge el paisaje en una luz mística e irreal, se rinde uno ante la fascinación de Australia, de este país increíble de contrastes y superlativos.

Pero también con su fauna y flora únicas seduce la fabulosa selva de Nueva Zelanda, cuya tercera parte es espacio natural protegido y que produce el efecto de ser una tierra mágica atemporal.

El exotismo de las pintorescas lagunas, de las exuberantes flores tropicales de polinesia, aparta mientras tanto en aparente eterno, sereno sosiego, la levedad del ser.

Los exclusivos hoteles, refugios y centros turísticos elegidos aquí, son complementos sublimes de estos destinos de viaje extraordinarios. Estilo, confort y técnica relacionan ciudades históricas, selvas arcaicas o sueños de naturaleza lejanos con la modernidad de nuestro tiempo, logran sobrecogedores panoramas y preservan al mismo tiempo el romanticismo singular de estos refugios. En el campo de fuerza entre una extraordinaria, moderna arquitectura o cascos históricos y un interior juguetón o una elegancia de líneas rectas, estas casas de huéspedes detrás de sus fachadas cumplen con las expectativas de sus exigentes clientes. Este libro lo ayudará a hacer realidad sus sueños presentándole los más bonitos hoteles de esta atractiva región.

Constanze Junker

Introduzione

Australia, Nuova Zelanda, i Mari del Sud – paesaggi belli da togliere il fiato nell'emisfero sud, ognuno, a modo suo, un luogo da sognare e desiderare. E per molta gente è il paradiso dall'altra parte del mondo.

Davvero vale la pena di intraprendere il lungo viaggio fino a lì. Foreste pluviali tropicali e deserti disabitati, spiagge infinite e la più grande barriera di corallo del mondo, fattorie solitarie, cittadine abbandonate dai cercatori d'oro e metropoli operose: verso sera, quando fra le quattro e le cinque il sole si immerge nel paesaggio come per *Magic Hour*, avvolto da una luce mitica, quasi irreale, si viene totalmente sedotti dal fascino dell'Australia, questo incredibile Paese dei contrasti e dei superlativi.

Ma ciò che più incanta, con la sua flora e la sua fauna uniche, è il luogo selvaggio fiabesco della Nuova Zelanda, che è zona protetta per un terzo della sua estensione ed ha l'aspetto di un luogo magico, fuori dal tempo.

Invece le pittoresche lagune esotiche, i sontuosi fiori tropicali della Polinesia ti portano via in una serena tranquillità apparentemente ininterrotta, la leggerezza dell'essere.

Gli hotel esclusivi e selezionati, gli alberghi ed i resort sono sublimi complementi di queste straordinarie destinazioni. Lo stile, la comodità e la tecnologia uniscono le città storiche, le foreste arcaiche o i sogni di una natura lontana con la modernità del nostro tempo, danno vita a panorami mozzafiato e mantengono allo stesso tempo il singolare romanticismo di questi luoghi. Nel conflitto fra l'architettura straordinaria e moderna o gli edifici storici e gli interni frivoli o l'eleganza dalle linee pulite dietro la facciata, queste residenze soddisfano le aspettative degli ospiti più esigenti. Questo volume vi aiuterà a realizzare i vostri sogni presentando gli hotel più belli di questa regione ricca di attrattiva.

Constanze Junker

The Buckland – Studio Retreat

McCormack's Lane
Buckland Valley
Victoria 3741
Australia
Phone: +61 / 3 / 57 56 23 83
www.thebuckland.com.au

Price category: $$
Rooms: 4 studios, 1 luxury chalet
Facilities: The Buckland Café, bush walking, golf, mountain biking, skiing
Services: Internet, DVD library, phone
Located: Close to Bright Victoria, Mt. Buffalo National Park & the snowfields of Victoria's High Country
Map: No. 1
Style: Modern country chic
What's special: Romantic, idyllic, environmentally sensitive: 5 studios individually designed in the contemporary Australian style and located in a private natural terrain provide the ideal basis for trekking tours and animal observations. More than 30 species of bird can be observed in the immediate surroundings.

The Byron at Byron Resort and Spa

77–97 Broken Head Road
Byron Bay
New South Wales 2481
Australia
Phone: +61 / 2 / 66 39 20 00
Fax: +61 / 2 / 66 39 21 99
www.thebyronatbyron.com.au

Price category: $$$
Rooms: 92 suites
Facilities: Day spa, restaurant, pool, tennis court, gymnasium, daily yoga
Services: Each suite contains a kitchen, separate lounge and dining area, plasma TV as well as 2 enclosed balconies
Located: 5 min south of Byron Bay
Map: No. 2
Style: Modern country chic
What's special: Situated within a sub tropical rainforest and moments from the beach, this stylish resort offers the perfect place to relax and unwind. Daytime activities include swimming pool, day spa, beach, gym, tennis and rainforest walks on endless timber boardwalks, as well as complimentary yoga every morning.

Olive Grove Retreat

Travers Lane
Heathcote
Victoria 3523
Australia
Phone: +61 / 04 03 87 69 88
www.olivegroveretreat.com

Price category: $$$
Rooms: 1 luxury guesthouse
Facilities: Swimming pool, fireplace
Services: Arrangements of private opera, massage
and a cleaning lady are optional
Located: 50 min from Melbourne Airport,
90 min from Melbourne
Map: No. 3
Style: Romantic countrystyle
What's special: Pure privacy: In the middle of the
Australian bush, couples experience an exclusive
coddling by a service team, cook and masseur in this
romantic guesthouse with its refreshing stylistic blend
of French furniture, Italian fabrics and oriental
accessories.

Crown Promenade Hotel

8 Whiteman Street
Southbank
Melbourne
Victoria 3006
Australia
Phone: +61 / 3 / 92 92 66 88
Fax: +61 / 3 / 92 92 53 97
www.crownpromenade.com.au

Price category: $$$
Rooms: 465 guest rooms, 18 studios and 3 suites
Facilities: Restaurant, bar, indoor infinity pool,
2 outdoor deck areas, steam rooms and gymnasium
Services: Tea and coffee making facilities, iron and
ironing board, Internet access
Located: In Melbourne's Southbank entertainment
precinct
Map: No. 4
Style: Modern classic
What's special: In the heart of bustling Southbank this
modern city hotel has its own passageway connecting
it to the exciting Crown Entertainment Complex for art
and nonstop entertainment. On the roof: infinity pool and
fitness center with fantastic views over Port Phillip Bay or
the Yarra River.

Hotel Lindrum

26 Flinders Street
Melbourne
Victoria 3000
Australia
Phone: +61 / 3 / 96 68 11 11
Fax: +61 / 3 / 96 68 11 99
www.hotellindrum.com.au

Price category: $$
Rooms: 59 rooms and suites
Facilities: Restaurant, bar, dining room, conference room, library, billard room, lounge with open fireplace
Services: Babysitting services, tea and coffee making facilities
Located: In the center of Melbourne
Map: No. 5
Style: Chic and stylish interior
What's special: With a love for detail, architects and designers melded the classic details of the historical building with a sophisticated, stylish interior. This elegant boutique hotel sees itself as the home for modern travelers amidst the hustle and bustle of this cosmopolitan city.

The Prince

2 Acland Street
St Kilda
Victoria 3182
Australia
Phone: +61 / 3 / 95 36 11 11
www.theprince.com.au

Price category: $$$
Rooms: 40 guest rooms
Facilities: Restaurant Circa, 2 bars, café, bakery, spa, running track along the beach
Services: Babysitting service
Located: In St Kilda, a cosmopolitan area minutes away from Melbourne's best beaches, trendy shops and restaurants
Map: No. 6
Style: Urban chic
What's special: The functional art deco façade almost hides the fact that inside this boutique hotel the interplay of art and design is reminiscent of a gallery. In the romantic restaurant Circa, creations of one of Melbourne's best cuisine are served. And the beach is only a few minutes walk away.

SHALLOW | NO DIVING | Depth 0.3m

and the Royal Botanic Garden, this villa built in 1902 in the Italian style combines behind its elaborately designed façade an exciting mix of traditional and postmodern elements into an elegant boutique hotel.

Moonlight Head Private Lodge

35 Parkers Access Road
Yuulong
Victoria 3237
Australia
Phone: +61 / 3 / 52 37 52 08
www.moonlighthead.com

Price category: $$$
Rooms: 3 Lodges, each sleeps up to eight people in 4 bedrooms
Facilities: Full service all inclusive accommodation for couples, groups & families
Services: 24 h room service
Located: 3-h drive from Melbourne along the Great Ocean Road
Map: No. 8
Style: Modern minimalist interior
What's special: Glenn Murcutt designed environmental sensitive lodges, with a European flair. Overlooking the Great Southern Ocean, where it is just you and the Kangaroos. Among the highlights are local trips to the 12 Apostles, the famous Great Ocean Walk, horseback riding, breakfast with Spike the koala or canoeing with the Platypus.

Diamant Boutique Hotel Canberra

15 Edinburgh Avenue
Canberra
Australian Capital Territory 2601
Australia
Phone: +61/2/61 75 22 22
Fax: +61/2/61 75 22 33
www.diamant.com.au

Price category: $$$
Rooms: 80
Facilities: Diamant Lounge Bar & Library, Parlour Wine Room, Du Jour Restaurant, Flint Dining Room & Bar
Services: Soma Day Spa, gym, personal fitness training, pilates
Located: In Canberra's first true urban village, on the Lake Burley Griffin
Map: No. 9
Style: Boutique
What's special: Located within the original Hotel Acton building, this historical and heritage listed site has been transformed into the NewActon Pavilion incorporating the Diamant Hotel and creating Canberra's first luxury boutique hotel. Designed by celebrated interior designer SJB Interiors, the Diamant Hotel features several restaurants & bars.

Voyages Wilson Island

The Great Barrier Reef
Queensland
Australia
Phone: +61 / 2 / 82 96 80 10
Fax: +61 / 2 / 92 99 21 03
www.wilsonisland.com

Price category: $$$$
Rooms: 6 permanent tents for a maximum of 12 guests,
open kitchen and lounge
Facilities: Glass bottom kayaks, bird watching
Services: All tents with reef & ocean outlooks
Located: In the north east of the Tropic of Capricorn,
approximately 72 km northeast the coast of Gladstone
and 15 km from nearby Heron Island
Map: No. 10
Style: Modern country chic
What's special: A maximum of 12 guests can lodge in
6 uber-chic designer-inspired, solar-energized tents
on the tiny coral cay of the Great Barrier Reef and, in
season, observe rare tortoises and their offspring in their
natural surroundings.

Limes Hotel

142 Constance Street
Fortitude Valley
Brisbane
Queensland 4006
Australia
Phone: +61 / 7 / 38 52 90 00
Fax: +61 / 7 / 38 52 90 99
www.limeshotel.com.au

Price category: $$$
Rooms: 21 rooms
Facilities: Roof top bar, roof top cinema
Services: Rooms feature 32-inch television with Foxtel cable, iPod dock, kitchenette
Located: In the hub of Brisbane's nightlife, 13 km from Brisbane Airport
Map: No. 11
Style: Urban chic
What's special: Modern, unfussy design hotel with warm atmosphere in Fortitude Valley, Brisbane's nightlife district with trendy cafés, shops, bars and restaurants. Stylish open-air bar on the roof, with open-air cinema from Monday to Wednesday. Some rooms have their own courtyard with hammock.

BLUE Sydney, A Taj Hotel

The Wharf at Woolloomooloo
6 Cowper Wharf Road
Sydney
New South Wales 2011
Australia
Phone: +61 / 2 / 93 31 90 00
Fax: +61 / 2 / 93 31 90 31
www.tajhotels.com/sydney

Price category: $$
Rooms: 100 guest rooms, including 36 stunning loft rooms
Facilities: BLUE Café, Water Bar, fitness center, outdoor sun deck
Services: 24 h 5-star service
Located: On the wharf at Woolloomooloo, Sydney, close to the harbor and shopping district
Map: No. 12
Style: Contemporary chic
What's special: Directly on Woolloomooloo pier, this boutique hotel in the heart of a lively luxury marina offers sensational views of the city's business and financial centers, the harbor and the Royal Botanical Garden. Traditional wood furnishings complement to the stylish-modern ambience.

Establishment

5 Bridge Lane
Sydney
New South Wales 2000
Australia
Phone: +61 / 2 / 92 40 31 00
Fax: +61 / 2 / 92 40 31 01
www.merivale.com

Price category: $$$
Rooms: 31 guest rooms, including 2 penthouse suites
Facilities: Restaurants, bars, private gym
Services: 24 h reception/concierge, 24 h room service, dry cleaning, access to a private gym, babysitting
Located: In the middle of Sydney's central business district, close to the harbor
Map: No. 13
Style: A luxurious boutique hotel, with a uniquely intimate feel
What's special: Elegant rooms and two stylish penthouses both with a unique and personal atmosphere. This luxury boutique hotel with its bars and restaurants is a meeting point between Sydney Harbour, Opera House and Botanical Garden.

Voyages Longitude 131°

Yulara Drive
Ayers Rock 0872
Yulara
Northern Territory
Australien
Phone: +61 / 2 / 82 96 80 10
Fax: +61 / 2 / 92 99 21 03
www.longitude131.com.au

Price category: $$$$
Rooms: 15 private luxury tents
Facilities: Restaurant, bar, pool, private touring, camel rides, dining under the stars, sunrise walk
Services: Complimentary airport transfers
Located: On a sand dune close to the border of the World Heritage listed Uluru-Kata Tjuta National Park, just 6 km from Ayers Rock Airport
Map: No. 14
Style: Modern design
What's special: White, tent-like roofs span luxurious, eco-sensitive studio suites in the Outback from which the exquisitely colorful play of light on the Uluru can be observed. For the evening there are romantic dinners under a sparkling starry sky. Numerous guided tours. Handicapped accessible furnishings possible on demand.

The Lodge at Tarraleah

Wild River Road
Tarraleah
Tasmania 7140
Australia
Phone: +61 / 3 / 62 89 11 99
Fax: +61 / 3 / 62 89 01 36
www.tarraleahlodge.com

Price category: $$$
Rooms: 9 deluxe rooms and suites
Facilities: Restaurant, bar, spa & health center, adventure guides, birding and tiger hunts
Services: 4-course Tasmanian specialty gourmet dinner and chef cooked breakfast included, 300 wines and over 200 malts, private parking
Located: On an elevated highland plateau, on the edge of the wilderness, 1,5-h drive from Hobart
Map: No. 15
Style: Luxury
What's special: Authentically designed luxury suites in the style of the Tasmanian pioneers. Relaxing in cedar bathtubs, guests enjoy breathtaking views of the original wilderness. One of the top twenty fishing lodges of the world. Fishing courses possible.

Cradle Mountain Lodge

4038 Cradle Mountain Road
Cradle Mountain
Tasmania 7306
Australia
Phone: +61 / 3 / 64 92 21 00
Fax: +61 / 2 / 92 99 21 03
www.cradlemountainlodge.com.au

Price category: $$
Rooms: 86 individual timber cabins
Facilities: Restaurant, bars, meeting rooms, trout fishing, native animal night viewing tour, Waldheim Alpine Spa
Services: Babysitting, children's dinner and supervised activities
Located: 81 km from Devonport, close to the Cradle Mountain and the Lake St Clair National Park
Map: No. 16
Style: Rustic elegance
What's special: Luxury spa at the edge of the Tasmanian Wilderness World Heritage Area. Only natural cosmetics produced in Australia and Tasmania are used in the spa. Over 20 hiking paths around Cradle Mountain and Dove Lake provide additional ways to relax in this natural paradise.

The Islington Hotel

321 Davey Street
Hobart
Tasmania 7000
Australia
Phone: +61 / 3 / 62 20 21 23
Fax: +61 / 3 / 62 20 21 24
www.islingtonhotel.com

Price category: $$$
Rooms: 11
Facilities: Outside glass pavilion with open fire &
BBQ facility, drawing room, extensive wine cellar
Services: Private dinners on request
Located: In the Dress Circle of Hobart, 5 min from
Hobart's city center
Map: No. 17
Style: Luxury boutique hotel
What's special: Built in 1847, the charm of the time of
origin is mirrored in the architecture and in 5 rooms with
original furnishings. 6 further rooms were designed by
the award-winning bureau of Morris Nunn & Associates.
The artistically landscaped garden was designed by the
well-known garden designer Andrew Pfeiffer. Library with
collection of the writings of Louisa A. Meredith.

鶴

The Henry Jones Art Hotel

25 Hunter Street
Hobart
Tasmania 7000
Australia
Phone: +61/3/62 10 77 00
Fax: +61/3/62 10 77 55
www.thehenryjones.com

Price category: $$
Rooms: 56
Facilities: Restaurants and bars, spa
Services: All rooms feature original artworks, high-speed Internet connectivity, LCD TV and DVD
Located: On Hobart's waterfront
Map: No. 18
Style: Boutique design hotel
What's special: Accommodated in a jam factory from the 1820's in the harbor of Hobart, the hotel combines the style of Tasmania's wealthy mercantile tradition with ultra modern charm. Furnished with over 250 works of art testifying Tasmania's vibrant art scene, furniture by renowned designer Kevin Perkins and hyper modern baths with overflowing bath tubes.

The Henry Jones Art Hotel

Eagles Nest

60 Tapeka Road
Russel
Bay of Islands
New Zealand
Phone: +61 / 9 / 4 03 83 33
Fax: +61 / 9 / 4 03 88 80
www.eagelsnest.co.nz

Price category: $$$
Rooms: 5 luxury villas
Facilities: Private heated horizon edged lap pool, Jacuzzi, own resident personal trainer and spa therapists
Services: Each villa features plasma televisions, home cinemas, gourmet kitchens and WiFi
Located: Seaside, North Island, New Zealand
Map: No. 19
Style: Contemporary design
What's special: 5 multiple award-winning modern luxury villas on their own peninsula high above the Bay of Islands, 4 of them with their own infinity pool. On request, a team of cooks prepares fresh fish and seafood dinners in the villas.

The Farm at Cape Kidnappers

448 Clifton Road
Te Awanga
Hawke's Bay
New Zealand
Phone: +64/6/8 75 19 00
Fax: +64/6/8 75 19 01
www.capekidnappers.com

Price category: $$$
Rooms: 22 suites and 1 four bedroom owner's cottage
Facilities: Swimming pool, quad & mountain biking, spa, hot air ballooning & helicopter flights, wine cellar
Services: WiFi, LCD TV, DVD, CD with iPod connection
Located: On the east coast of the North Island, in New Zealand's premier wine region, Hawke's Bay
Map: No. 20
Style: Rustic chic
What's special: Set on a 6,000-acre working sheep and cattle farm, Cape Kidnappers is home to the world's largest mainland gannet colony. Spacious cottages, each with breathtaking views, open to large porches overlooking a stunning Pacific panorama. Home to the recently voted best golf course in the world by the England's Daily Telegraph newspaper.

The Lodge at Kauri Cliffs

Matauri Bay Road
Matauri Bay
Northland
New Zealand
Phone: +64 / 9 / 4 07 00 10
Fax: +64 / 9 / 4 07 00 61
www.kauricliffs.com

Price category: $$
Rooms: 16 deluxe suites, 6 suites & 1 two-bedroom owner's cottage
Facilities: Spa & fitness center, swimming pool, 3 beaches, scuba diving, sea kayaking, horseback riding
Services: Room service available on request
Located: On 6,000 acres near Matauri Bay, Northland
Map: No. 21
Style: Colonial elegance
What's special: Kauri Cliffs affords spectacular 180-degree views of the Pacific Ocean. Cape Brett and the offshore Cavalli Islands are part of the panorama which can be viewed from the verandas, living room and the guest cottages. Luxurious spa nestled at the edge of a native totara forest and overlooking a verdant fern glen and winding stream.

River Birches Lodge

19 Koura Street
Turangi
Taupo
New Zealand
Phone: +64 / 7 / 3 86 04 45
Fax: +64 / 7 / 3 86 04 42
www.riverbirches.co.nz

Price category: $$$
Rooms: 3 guest rooms
Facilities: Skiing on Mount Ruapehu, golf course, white water rafting, Tongariro crossing, fitness room
Services: iPod mini sound system, WiFi
Located: In a superb New Zealand location, close to the renowned Tongariro Crossing, only footsteps away from the world famous fly fishing on the Tongariro River
Map: No. 22
Style: East meets West
What's special: Straightforward elegance and stylish interior characterize this boutique lodge in the middle of a landscaped garden with old trees on the Tongariro River. In summer attract trout fishing and Tongariro crossing in the national park of that name, in winter ski tours on Mount Ruapehu.

Treetops Lodge

351 Kearoa Road RD1
Horohoro Rotorua
New Zealand
Phone: +64 / 7 / 3 33 20 66
Fax: +64 / 7 / 3 33 20 65
www.treetops.co.nz

Price category: $$$
Rooms: 4 suites, 8 villas
Facilities: Photographic safari, geocaching, trout fishing, horseback riding, hiking, mountain biking, eco safaris
Services: Fireplaces
Located: In the trout fishing capital of the world and famed therapeutic thermal region, Rotorua, New Zealand
Map: No. 23
Style: Rustic elegance
What's special: Sustainably operated luxury resort in the renowned therapeutic thermal region of Rotorua. Numerous guided safaris, waterfall hikes and helicopter flights over volcanoes and the breathtaking sierras are only some of the countless activities available.

Mollies on Tweed

6 Tweed Street
St Mary's Bay
Auckland
New Zealand
Phone: +64 / 9 / 3 76 34 89
Fax: +64 / 9 / 3 78 65 92
www.mollies.co.nz

Price category: $$$$
Rooms: 14 magnificently appointed luxury suites
Facilities: Cottage garden and intimate outdoor areas,
drawing room, cocktail bar, restaurant, spa, fitness room
Services: Each suite is very individual with its own
balcony and unique interior features, private dining
Located: In the exclusive inner city suburb of St Mary's
Bay in Auckland New Zealand, only 5-min drive from
Auckland City
Map: No. 24
Style: Modern country chic
What's special: Passionate opera fans with a love of
detail combined fine antiques with straight-lined modern
furniture into a romantic luxury hotel of sophisticated
elegance. Attractive, intimate cottage garden and library
for relaxation. Gourmet restaurant on the spot.

Mollies on Tweed

lies on Tweed

THE QUADRANT HOTEL AUCKLAND

10 Waterloo Quadrant
Auckland
New Zealand
Phone: +61/9/9 84 60 00
Fax: +61/9/9 84 60 01
www.thequadrant.com

Price category: $$
Rooms: 250 studios, one- and two-bedroom apartments
Facilities: Quad Bar, Quad Kitchen, gymnasium, spa and sauna, valet car parking, meeting room, business center
Services: High-speed WiFi, LCD phone with voicemail and data ports, Sky-ready television, DVD player in every room, dry cleaning and foreign exchange
Located: Close to Albert Park, Queen St. and entertainment venue Vector Arena. 5-min walk to the Sky Tower
Map: No. 25
Style: Hip, funky, modern, passionate and sassy
What's special: Auckland's hippest 4-star experience. Simple living in comfortable apartment-style rooms and value for money is why The Quadrant stands alone as a affordable hip Hotel. Balcony and kitchen complete all apartments.

Delamore Lodge

83 Delamore Drive
PO Box 572
Waiheke Island
New Zealand
Phone: +64 / 9 / 3 72 73 72
Fax: +64 / 9 / 3 72 73 82
www.delamorelodge.com

Price category: $$$
Rooms: 4 luxury guest suites
Facilities: Golf, diving, kayaking, fishing, sailing, Jacuzzi, sauna
Services: Each suite feature a private patio, open shower, DVD/CD entertainment system
Located: Into the hillside, one 100 m above the sheltered waters of Owhanake Bay on the northwestern tip of Waiheke Island, Auckland City
Map: No. 26
Style: Luxury lodge
What's special: This Mediterranean inspired, exquisite lodge whose different levels seamlessly overlap is enthroned almost 100 m above the sheltered Owhanake Bay. The cuisine is ambitious, with fresh products partly prepared from own vegetable and herb garden.

Whare Kea Lodge

Mt Aspiring Road
Wanaka 9343
New Zealand
Phone: +64 / 3 / 4 43 14 00
Fax: +64 / 3 / 4 43 92 00
www.wharekealodge.com

Price category: $$$
Rooms: 2 master suites and 4 double rooms
Facilities: Massage room, Jacuzzi, billiard & TV lounge room, heli-skiing, golf, fly fishing, winery tours
Services: Every room has direct access to the sundeck, coffee and tea making facilities, WiFi
Located: Near the township of Wanaka, on 70 acres of private farmland with direct access to Lake Wanaka
Map: No. 27
Style: Contemporary
What's special: Laid-back luxury on Lake Wanaka in the Southern Alps. Many pastime activities on land, water and in the air possible, including salmon catching and heli-skiing. A personal guide is available for mountain tours. The chalet in the high alpine range of the Buchanan Mountains is only accessible by helicopter.

Blanket Bay

PO Box 35
Glenorchy 9350
New Zealand
Phone: +64 / 3 / 4 41 01 15
Fax: +64 / 3 / 4 42 94 41
www.blanketbay.com

Price category: $$
Rooms: 5 intimate lodge rooms, 7 suites
Facilities: Scenic helicopter flights, hiking, horseback riding, mountain biking, heli-fishing, heli-skiing
Services: All rooms are equipped with complimentary high-speed Internet connection, TVs and DVDs
Located: At the north end of Lake Wakatipu, 35 min from Queenstown, 50 min from the airport
Map: No. 29
Style: Rustic elegance
What's special: Small exclusive lodge backed by majestic mountains at the northern end of Lake Wakatipu. Countless leisure activities like fishing, riding, heli-skiing, canyoning, hiking and flying over the World Heritage Fiordland National Park.

Eichardt's Private Hotel

Marine Parade
PO Box 1340
Queenstown
New Zealand
Phone: +64 / 3 / 4 41 04 50
Fax: +64 / 3 / 4 41 04 40
www.eichardtshotel.co.nz

Price category: $$$$
Rooms: 5 hotel suites, 4 lakefront cottage suites
Facilities: Bar, lounge, restaurant
Services: Babysitting and child care services, Internet access – dial-up, WiFi in all suites
Located: On the waterfront of Queenstown's pristine Lake Wakatipu
Map: No. 28
Style: Contemporary elegance
What's special: Located in a historic building at the lakefront of Queenstown's café and restaurant district, the hotel offers opulent suites in contemporary elegance. Antiques and modern features create a cozy atmosphere in all rooms equipped with fireplaces. The iconic House Bar offers some of the area's finest cocktails and cuisine.

Jean-Michel Cousteau Fiji Islands Resort

Savusavu
Vanua Levu
Fiji Islands
Phone +1 / 415 / 7 88 57 94
Fax +1 / 415 / 7 88 01 50
www.fijiresort.com

Price category: $$$$
Rooms: 25 bures, including 1 grand villa
Facilities: 4 swimming pools, tennis court, spa, diving, free daily kids Bula Club
Services: Organic garden that grows many vegetables, herbs and fruits for our guests
Located: On Vanua Levu near Savusavu. Savusavu Airport is a 1-h flight from Nadi International Airport
Map: No. 30
Style: Luxury
What's special: Located on the island of Vanua Levu, traditional thatched-roof bures are nestled in a 6-ha coconut grove with a view over Savusavu Bay. The marine biologist leads snorkeling and diving excursions and coral reef flat walks. The Fijian naturalist leads excursions to the rainforest and to a native Fijian village.

Royal Davui Island Resort

PO Box 3171
Lami
Fiji Islands
Phone: +67 / 9 / 3 30 70 90
Fax: +67 / 9 / 3 31 15 00
www.royaldavui.com

Price category: $$$$
Rooms: 16 exquisitely appointed houses
Facilities: Restaurant, bar, scuba diving, snorkelling, kayaking
Services: Breakfast and dinner on your private dining deck
Located: Off the tip of Beqa Island in the beautiful Beqa Lagoon
Map: No. 31
Style: Elegant tropical design
What's special: Multiple award-winning luxury resort in the breathtaking Vale Beqa Lagoon; reserved for adults only. This private island is located in one of the best diving regions of the Fiji Islands whose special attractions are soft coral diving and shark diving in Fiji Islands first Shark Reef Marine Reserve only 45 min away.

Royal Davui Island Resort   173

Vatulele Island Resort Managed by Six Senses

Vatulele Island
Fiji Island
Phone: +67 / 9 / 6 72 03 00
Fax: +67 / 9 / 6 72 00 62
www.sixsenses.com

Price category: $$$$
Rooms: 19 villas
Facilities: Gold Palm PADI Dive Center, wine cellar, organic vegetable garden, restaurant plus private dining, excursions, water activities
Services: Spa treatments, Internet access, butlers, weddings
Located: 25-min flight from Nadi International Airport
Map: No. 32
Style: Tropical chic
What's special: Nestled on an expansive sand beach, the sustainably-built guesthouses offer generous personal space. 6 villas have their own pools while 2 large villas on the periphery of the resort have their own pools and personal butler service.

PO Box 15424
Wakaya Island
Fiji Islands
Phone: +67 / 9 / 3 44 81 28
Fax: +67 / 9 / 3 44 84 06
www.wakaya.com

Price category: $$$$
Rooms: 10 free-standing waterfront Fijian cottage suites
Facilities: Spa treatments, private beaches, beach picnics, golf course, sea kayaking, glass bottom boat tours
Services: In-room dining, high-speed Internet access
Located: On Wakaya Island, surrounded by a protected coral reef
Map: No. 33
Style: Luxury boutique hotel
What's special: 2,200-acre private island with eco-friendly luxury lodgings erected in unspoiled nature. The exquisite cuisine, specializing in Pacific meals, is based on regional organic products. A 9-hole golf course, tennis and croquet court and 24 km of hiking paths round out the pastime possibilities.

Four Seasons Resort Bora Bora

Motu Tehotu – BP 547
98730 Bora Bora
French Polynesia
Phone: +68/9/60 31 30
Fax: +68/9/60 31 71
www.fourseasons.com/borabora

Price category: $$$$
Rooms: 100 overwater bungalows, 7 beachfront villas
Facilities: 4 restaurants and bars, full-service spa, fitness center, separate island for teens Kids For All Seasons with its own pool, lagoonarium
Services: Babysitting service
Located: Faa'a International Airport 45 min, Bora Bora Airport 15 min by boat
Map: No. 34
Style: Polynesian chic
What's special: Exotic over-the-water suites and beach villas combine ultra modern comfort with typical Polynesian furnishings. Arii Moana indulges you with choice seafood specialties. Besides a variety of water sports, leisure activities include jeep safaris, shark and ray feeding.

Motu Tape – BP 190
98730 Bora Bora
French Polynesia
Phone: +68/9/60 51 51
Fax: +68/9/60 51 52
www.lemeridien-borabora.com

Price category: $$$$
Rooms: 99 guest rooms
Facilities: 4 restaurants, bar, lagoonarium, catamaran cruise, parasailing, jet skiing, aqua safari, shark and ray feeding, deep sea fishing
Services: Laundry service, babysitting service, DVD library
Located: On one of the most scenic Motu (islets), facing the Otemanu Mountain, on the edge of an azure lagoon
Map: No. 35
Style: modern tropical design
What's special: Located on the vehicle-free island of Motu in one of Polynesia's loveliest lagoons. In the tortoise reserve Le Méridien guests learn what there is to know about tortoises—they can swim with them in the lagoon or "adopt" them. The traditional Kaïnalu canoe has only been put to use again here and is available for excursions.

Intercontinental Resort Tahiti

Point Tahiti
Po Box 6014
Papeete, 00000
French Polynesia
Phone: +68/9/86 51 10
Fax: +68/9/86 51 30
www.ichotelsgroup.com/
intercontinental/en/gb/
locations/tahiti

Price category: $$$$
Rooms: 260 guest rooms, 1 suite, executive suites
Facilities: Restaurant, 2 bars, aquatica dive center, lagoonarium, private beach, 2 pools, tennis courts, 12 ha garden, 12 meeting rooms
Services: Fully serviced meeting & function facilities are available indoors and outdoors
Located: Papeete's museums, shops, galleries, market and nightclubs are a short drive away
Map: No. 36
Style: Traditional Polynesian
What's special: This resort, maintained in the Polynesian style, is surrounded by a lush garden of almost 13 ha and has a private beach and its own lagoon. From August to October: Observation of humpback whales which come here to calve.

Intercontinental Resort Tahiti   207

Hilton Moorea Lagoon Resort & Spa

Papetoai
Moorea
French Polynesia
Phone: +68 / 9 / 55 11 11
Fax: +68 / 9 / 55 11 55
www.hilton.com

Price category: $$$$
Rooms: 54 overwater, 52 garden and beach bungalows
Facilities: Restaurant, Rotui Bar & Grill, The Eimeo Bar, The Toata Bar, tournament tennis courts, fitness facility
Services: Daily live entertainment troughout the resort starting at sunset
Located: Between two bays on heart-shaped Moorea
Map: No. 37
Style: Romantic luxury
What's special: Situated between Cook's Bay and Opunohu Bay, the typical Polynesian bungalows in warm colors of this familiar hotel are located in an exotic garden or above the water are. Through the floors of the water bungalows one can observe the tropical underwater world.

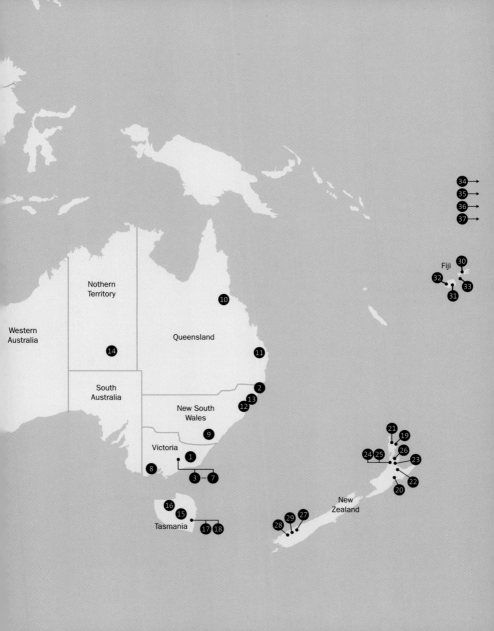

Western
Australia

Nothern
Territory

Queensland

South
Australia

New South
Wales

Victoria

Tasmania

New
Zealand

Fiji

1
2
3
7
8
9
10
11
12
13
14
15
16
17
18
19
20
21
22
23
24
25
26
27
28
29
30
31
32
33
34
35
36
37

Other titles by teNeues

ISBN 978-3-8327-9309-8

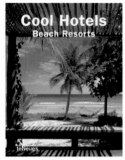

ISBN 978-3-8327-9274-9

ISBN 978-3-8327-9237-4

ISBN 978-3-8327-9247-3

ISBN 978-3-8327-9234-3

ISBN 978-3-8327-9308-1

ISBN 978-3-8327-9243-5

ISBN 978-3-8327-9230-5

ISBN 978-3-8327-9248-0

Size: **15 x 19 cm**, 6 x 7 ½ in., 224 pp., **Flexicover**, c. 200 color photographs,
Text: English / German / French / Spanish / Italian
www.teneues.com

Other titles by teNeues

ISBN 978-3-8327-9238-1

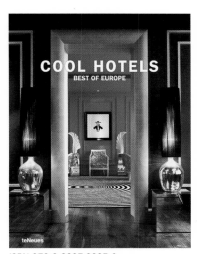

ISBN 978-3-8327-9235-0

Size: **25.6 x 32.6 cm**, 10 x 12⁷⁄₈ in., 396 pp., **Hardcover with jacket**, c. 650 color photographs,
Text: English / German / French / Spanish / Italian
www.teneues.com

Other titles by teNeues

ISBN 978-3-8327-9293-0

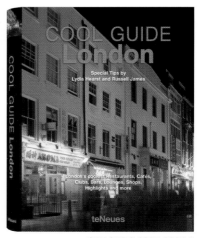

ISBN 978-3-8327-9294-7

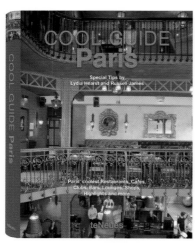

ISBN 978-3-8327-9295-4

ISBN 978-3-8327-9296-1

Size: **15 x 19 cm**, 6 x 7 ½ in., 224 pp., **Flexicover**, c. 250 color photographs,
Text: English / German / French / Spanish
www.teneues.com